Craft Workshop

Festival Decorations

Anne Civardi & Penny King

A & C Black · London

Designed by
Edward Kinsey

Illustrated by
Lindy Norton

Photography by
Steve Shott

Children's work by
Emily Ashworth, Emma Carrington-Brook, Amber Civardi, Charlotte Downham,
Lucy Figgis, James Jarman, Emma Loraine-Smith, Alice Masson-Taylor,
India Masson-Taylor, Georgina Mew, Victoria Moss, Archie Parrack,
Susie Roberts, Georgina Smith, Jessie Stratton, Florence Turner

First published in 1998 by
A & C Black
35 Bedford Row, London WC1R 4JH

Created by
Thumbprint Books

Copyright © 1998 Thumbprint Books

A CIP catalogue record for this book is available from the British Library

ISBN: 0-7136-4810-4 (Hbk)
ISBN: 0-7136-4811-2 (Pbk)

Printed in Hong Kong by Wing King Tong Co Ltd

Cover photograph: This Tree of Life comes from Mexico. Every year in November, on the Day of the Dead,
Mexicans place these candlesticks on family graves and light the candles to keep the spirits of the dead happy.

Contents

World festivals

Since ancient times, people all over the world have gathered together to celebrate important events, festivals and holidays. Many of these festivals are based on religion or tradition. They may celebrate the arrival of the New Year, the end of a long cold winter, harvest time, birth, marriage or death.

Throughout the year, people of all religions in every corner of the world have something to celebrate.

At Christmas, Christians celebrate the birth of Jesus. Easter is the time when they remember His death and the day He rose from the dead.

At the Hindu springtime festival of Holi, people run through the streets and throw buckets of coloured water over each other.

People decorate their homes, have huge feasts, set off fireworks and fly colourful flags. They dance and sing in large processions, wearing exotic costumes and masks.

Buddhist monks in Tibet perform a special dance to bring in the New Year. They wear fearsome masks to drive away evil spirits.

Guardian Deity Mask, Tibet, The Horniman Museum London

This book tells you about many of these fascinating occasions, both strange and spectacular.

You can learn all about the old Chinese tradition of bringing in spring with bright and colourful whirling windmills, and why Japanese families fly colourful carp banners, like these, outside their homes on Boys' day.

You can also find out about a unique competition held each year in Krakow, Poland, to build the best Nativity scene, and about the Hindu Festival of Lights, known as *Diwali*.

Inspired by the colours, clothes, splendour and objects used in these celebrations, children have made festival decorations like the ones below. Borrow their ideas to create some exciting ones of your own.

Tools and techniques

To make the decorations in this book, you'll need to collect bits and pieces, such as old shoe and cereal boxes, cardboard rolls, scraps of material, wool, raffia, shiny sweet wrappers, sequins, ribbon, ice-lolly sticks and corks.

You may also need to buy a few things from a craft shop or department store.

Paints

Ready-mixed poster paints can be used for many of the projects, but you might like to try acrylic paints. These cost a little more, but are brighter and shinier than other paints. You will also need fabric paints.

Fabrics

Felt is the easiest fabric to work with as it doesn't fray, comes in bright colours and can be bought in small amounts. If you don't feel like sewing, you can glue felt pieces together.

Scissors

Use pinking shears, scissors with zig-zag edges, to stop fabrics from fraying too much.

Glue

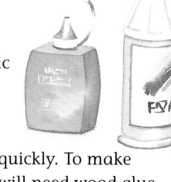

For many projects, you will need fabric glue or PVA glue. PVA glue can also be used instead of varnish as it dries quickly. To make bread dough, you will need wood glue.

Stuffing

Cotton wool is perfect for stuffing dolls and other shapes. You can also use newspaper or fabric pieces.

Papier mâché

Put some flour and PVA glue in a mixing bowl. Add enough water to make a mixture, about as thick as creamy yoghurt.

Tear sheets of newspaper into small pieces. Smooth a thick layer of the gooey mixture over the shape you are covering with papier mâché, such as a balloon or an orange. Cover it with four layers of newspaper strips. Finish off with a layer of the gooey mixture and leave it to harden.

Sewing

The simplest stitch to do is a running stitch. Thread a needle and tie a knot in the end. Pin two pieces of fabric together. Push the needle through both layers of fabric and out again, as shown. Make another stitch a little distance from the first one. Repeat this. When you have finished, make four or five stitches on top of each other to stop your sewing from coming undone.

Hemming

Turn over about 2 cm of fabric and do a running stitch close to the edge, as shown.

Cutting fabric shapes

To cut two identical fabric shapes, first draw a pattern on a piece of paper and cut it out.

Fold some fabric in half and pin the paper pattern on to it, making sure you pin through both layers. Carefully cut through both layers of fabric around the edge of the pattern.

Making bread dough

Cut the crusts off six or seven pieces of white sliced bread. Crumble them with your fingers. Put the crumbs in a mixing bowl and add some wood glue. Knead it into a thick dough. Add two tablespoons of talcum powder and knead it into the mixture. Put your bread dough decorations into the freezer to harden.

Making eyeholes in a mask

Put the mask up to your face. Ask a friend to draw circles on it, in roughly the position where your eyes are. Ask an adult to cut out these eye holes with sharp scissors.

Clay

Knead self-hardening clay until it is warm and flexible before you start to mould it. If you want to add extra pieces on to a model, such as the ears on the clay elephant lamp (see page 10), score both pieces, wet them with water and press them firmly together.

Smooth the clay with your fingers, so that the join doesn't show.

New Year

People the world over celebrate New Year with parties, dancing and music. It is a time for making resolutions to live a better life and for thinking about the future.

Hindus mark the start of their New Year in October or November with a Festival of Lights, known as *Diwali*. To welcome visitors and friends, they clean their houses and decorate them with glitter and tinsel.

They place little clay lamps, called *divas*, in their windows and outside their front doors. This is to attract Lakshmi, the goddess of wealth, whom they hope will visit their homes and bless them with a prosperous new year.

The Chinese New Year falls between late January and the middle of February. At this time, Chinese children receive little red and gold packets containing money known as 'lucky money'.

They may also be given special dolls, dressed in red and gold, clasping money packets in their hands. The Chinese believe that red and gold are lucky colours.

In Japan, people hang fans around their doors to bring them good luck in the coming year.

For centuries, fans have been an important accessory for both Japanese men and women. There are two kinds. The ones that fold are called *uchiwas*, those that don't fold are called *sensus*.

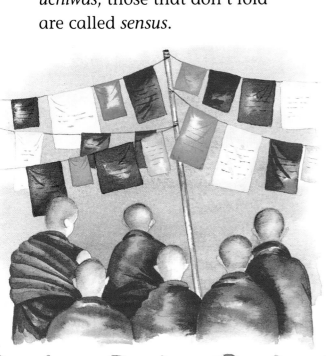

New Year is an important time for Buddhists. For 15 days in February, Tibetans celebrate their biggest festival, called *Losar*, when they remember Buddha. They paint their homes and hang up strings of colourful prayer flags, called Losar bunting. Each flag has a prayer or wish written on it.

Happy New Year

Welcome in the New Year with these bright and cheerful festival decorations.

Little lamps

Mould some self-hardening terracotta clay into an elephant or small bowl, like those on page 8. Leave them to dry. Use poster paints and a gold marker pen to decorate them with patterns. Glue on lengths of braid or coloured ribbon. Put a candle or night-light in each lamp.

Lucky money packets and dolls

Fold a rectangle of coloured card in half and glue two edges together to make a money packet. Draw patterns on it with a gold felt-tip pen.

Cut out two dolls exactly the same shape from red felt (see page 7). Glue a felt face, money packet, shoes, hair, hands and braid belt on one doll shape. Stitch on eyes, a nose, a mouth and lines to show where the arms are. Put the two doll shapes together and sew around the edges, leaving a small gap. Stuff the doll with cotton wool and sew up the gap.

Bright bunting

Use pinking shears to cut out lots of plain fabric rectangles. Turn over the short edge of each flag about 2 cm and hem it (see page 7). Pin a safety pin on to the end of a long piece of thin coloured rope and thread it through each flag. Hang up the string of flags in your room.

Fabulous fans

Cut a rectangle shape out of stiff white paper. Draw a Japanese-looking tree and patterns on the fan with felt-tip pens.

Leave the background white, or colour it with a felt-tip pen. When it is dry, fold the fan in a concertina and pinch the folds at one end together. Paint an ice-lolly stick black and tape it on to the back of the pinched folds.

Spring

In many parts of the world, spring is the time to celebrate the end of the long, dark days of winter. Flowers and leaves begin to grow and animals have their young. Spring is an exciting season when people celebrate new life.

Fabergé egg, The Royal Collection © Her Majesty the Queen

Eggs have been a sign of new life for many centuries. This beautiful egg was made by the famous Russian jeweller, Carl Fabergé. He created it in 1914 for Tsar Nicolas II of Russia to give to his wife, the Tsarina, as an Easter present.

The egg is made from gold, platinum, green, pink and white enamel and set with hundreds of precious diamonds, emeralds and rubies. Hidden inside, in a gold, diamond and pearl frame, is a picture of the Tsarina's five children.

Each spring, Christians around the world celebrate Easter. On the Saturday before Easter, people in Poland decorate real or wooden eggs. They are covered with delicate and beautiful patterns.

On Easter Sunday morning, Polish people decorate their breakfast tables with these eggs. They add green branches, pussy willows, and animals made from candy or an almond and sugar paste.

The Yaqui Indians of southern Arizona, USA, celebrate Christian Easter stories with dances. Some of the dancers wear painted masks made of paper or animal skins. They carry wooden swords or daggers. Other dancers wear head-dresses decorated with paper flowers and ribbons. They shake rattles made from dried gourds. Once the celebrations are over, the Yaqui burn the masks and weapons in a big fire.

At the Ch'ing-ming festival in Hong Kong, children welcome spring with shiny paper windmills which whirl around as they catch the wind.

Families take picnics to the countryside and visit their ancestors' tombs. Here they weed and tidy up the graves and burn red paper money as an offering to the dead.

Step into spring

Create an Easter egg fit for a Queen and some painted eggs to decorate your breakfast table on Easter day. Make noisy rattles and shiny windmills to welcome the spring.

Exotic egg

Cover a small blown-up balloon with papier mâché (see page 6). Leave a small opening at the bottom where the balloon is tied. When the papier mâché is hard, burst the balloon. Papier mâché over the opening. When it is dry, paint the egg a bright colour. Glue on sparkling decorations, such as sequins, glass beads, ribbon and shiny foil paper.

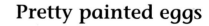

Pretty painted eggs

Ask an adult to help you hard-boil some eggs. When they are cool, paint them with poster or acrylic paints. When the eggs are dry, paint the eggs all over with colourful patterns.

Rowdy rattles

Cover an orange with a layer of cling film and then papier mâché (see page 6). When the papier mâché is hard, ask an adult to cut around the middle and remove the orange. Join the halves with gluey newspaper strips. Cut a hole in the bottom, big enough for a length of wooden dowelling.

Put dried peas through the hole and push in the handle. Use more gluey strips to hold the handle in place. When it is dry, paint the rattle a bright colour and decorate it with patterns. Glue ribbon around the handle.

Whirling windmills

Cut a square out of coloured foil paper. Draw two diagonal lines across the back. Carefully cut along the lines, stopping about 1 cm before the place where they cross. Turn over the square. Bend the four pointed ends into the centre and push a long pin through all four ends to keep them in place. Push the pin through a 1 cm length of drinking straw and then into the end of a long stick. Decorate the stick with paint and ribbons.

15

Harvest time

Autumn is the time when people give thanks for a good harvest and for the rain and sun which help their crops to grow.

Dogon mask © Edward Parker

The Dogon people from Mali, in west Africa, perform special masked dances to celebrate a good harvest. Some of the masks look like trees, or animals, such as antelopes, buffaloes or lizards.

This dancer is wearing a lizard mask over one metre high. During his energetic dance, he bends from the waist and scuffs the ground with the lizard's head to raise the dust.

At harvest festivals throughout Britain, church altars are decorated with flowers, fruit and vegetables. Sometimes, a loaf of bread, made in the shape of a wheat sheaf, is placed in the middle of the display. After a service of Thanksgiving, these gifts of food are given away to the poor or sick.

Each year, the people of Kerala, in southern India, celebrate a harvest festival, called *Onam*. Children pick flowers to decorate their homes and to weave into colourful patterns, called *pukalam*. In return, the elders give them new clothes to wear.

Corn dollies, woven from the last stalks and ears of grain, are still part of many harvest festivals. People believe that they will bring good luck and a successful harvest in the following year. This one, made of oats, silk, lace and ribbon, comes from Montenegro, in the Balkans.

Corn dolly, The Horniman Museum London

Wholesome harvest

Celebrate the end of harvest time by making your own animal mask, a tissue paper flower mat or a corn dolly.

Wild lizard mask

Paint a scary face on the bottom of a shoebox. Ask an adult to cut out holes for your eyes (see page 7) and a space for your neck. Cut out the shape of a lizard from stiff card. Paint it and then tape it, as shown, on to the top of the shoe box. Thread elastic through a hole in either side of the box, long enough to go around your head. Knot the ends.

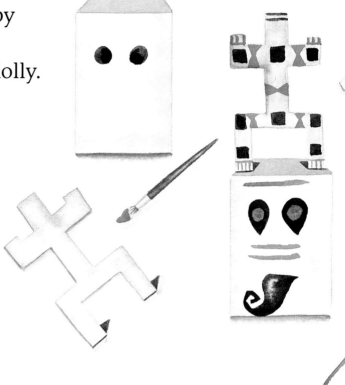

Glue lengths of wool, fabric or raffia to the top for wild hair. You could also glue on shells and feathers.

Fabulous flower mat

Cut out a round mat from loose-weave fabric. To make a fringe, cut short pieces of raffia and thread them, one by one, around the mat, 1 cm from the edge. Knot each one in place. For the flowers, cut large tissue circles of one colour and smaller circles of another colour.

Glue the middle of each of the small circles on to the middle of each large one. Lightly pinch the middles together. Glue the flowers in circles all over the mat with one big flower in the middle.

Corn dolly

For the body, make a thick bundle of dried grasses or raffia. Tie string tightly around the neck and hair to make a face. Separate two smaller bundles for the arms and tie a bow around each wrist. Decorate the dolly's body with lace, scraps of fabric, bows and tiny mirrors. Glue on coloured glass eyes.

Christmas

Every year, on Christmas Day, Christians celebrate
the birth of Jesus. Families worship in church,
sing carols and give each other presents.

This exquisite Nativity scene, showing the birth of Jesus is known as a *szopka*. It comes from Krakow in Poland and is based on a magnificent church there called Saint Mary's. The szopka is made from shiny paper and card.

Each December, a competition is held to see who can make the most beautiful szopka. Some are over 3 m high. The winners receive a prize, which is a great honour, and their szopkas are displayed in the Historical Museum.

In Sweden, the Festival of St Lucia on 13th December marks the beginning of Christmas celebrations. Dressed in white, girls wear wreaths of leaves on their heads and carry candles in honour of Lucia, the Christian saint of light. The girl who is chosen as the Lucia queen leads a procession from house to house wearing a crown of candles on her head.

This Christmas angel was made by the Shaker people of America. For over two hundred years, the Shakers have lived quietly in small communities. They are famous for their beautifully made crafts and furniture. They were first given the name *Shaker* in the 1700s, when members in England became excited during religious meetings. They would whirl and tremble, 'shaking' off their sins.

In Quito, Ecuador, women make these bread dough figures, called *figuras de masapan,* as colourful Christmas decorations. This art can be traced back to the small bread dolls that were made to celebrate All Souls' Day. These edible dolls, made in village bakeries, were placed in cemeteries as offerings to the hungry souls of the dead.

Christmas decorations

Build your own glimmering Nativity scene to remind you of the real reason for all the fun at Christmas. Make a cloth angel for the top of your Christmas tree, and bread dough decorations to hang from its branches.

Magical Nativity

Arrange different-sized boxes, such as used matchboxes or mini-cereal packets, to create a church with two spires. Cut a window out of one box. Use felt-tip pens to draw a picture of Joseph, Mary and Jesus on white card. Give them sequin haloes and then stick them inside the window.

Cover all the boxes with coloured foil sweet wrappers. Use glue and sticky tape to stick all the boxes together.

Glue a foil covered polystyrene ball on top of each spire. Decorate your Nativity scene with flags, a shooting star, a clock, mirrors and sequins.

Cloth angel

Cut out two identical figures from plain fabric (see page 7). Sew them together, leaving a small gap. Stuff the body and then sew up the gap.

Lie the angel on folded fabric. Draw on a dress shape and then cut it out through both layers of fabric. Sew up the side-seams and sleeves. Do the same to make the bloomers. Put the dress and bloomers on the angel. Tie ribbon around the wrists, neck and ankles. Glue heart shapes on the dress. Sew on thread hair and eyes.

Cut out two wing shapes. Sew them together and stuff them. Sew the wings on to the back of the angel.

Bread dough decorations

Flatten balls of bread dough (see page 7) into flat pancakes with your hands. Cut them into stockings, stars, snowmen or Christmas trees and smooth the edges with your fingers. Make a hole in the top of each shape. When they are dry, paint them bright colours and hang them on lengths of ribbon.

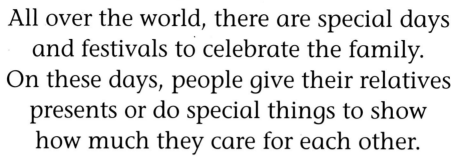

Family festivals

All over the world, there are special days
and festivals to celebrate the family.
On these days, people give their relatives
presents or do special things to show
how much they care for each other.

Boys' Day Carp © Eye Ubiquitous

On May 5th, a festival is held in Japan especially for boys. Outside their homes, parents fly giant cloth or paper kites, shaped like fish called carp. Each colourful kite represents a son, with the largest for the eldest boy.

Japanese people consider the carp to be the 'king of river fish' and respect it for its ability to swim upstream and overcome obstacles. They believe that it represents the strength and courage boys will need for their future lives.

In India, a festival for brothers and sisters, called *Raksha Bandhan*, takes place in August on the full moon day of *Shravana*. *Raksha* means 'protection' and *Bandan* means 'to tie'. In a special ceremony, a sister ties a thread bracelet, called a *rakhi*, on her brother's wrist to give him good luck. In return, the brother promises to look after his sister.

Mother's Day is held every year in Britain and North America. On this day, children give their mother flowers and cards to thank her for all the love and care she has given them. There is also a special day for fathers.

This colourful wool and stone prayer bundle was made by a North American Navaho Indian. It represents a husband and wife and their three children. The Navaho believe that if they put a prayer bundle in a sacred place in their home, the great spirit will watch over the family and bring it prosperity and good luck.

Family fun

These colourful presents, with their special meanings, make great gifts for your family and friends.

Dip a small sponge into a saucer of fabric paint. Press it on to the scales and tail to colour them. Print more patches with another colour. Leave the fish to dry.

Place the painted fish, paint side down, on top of the plain one. Pin them and then sew them together, except for the mouth. Turn 1 cm of fabric over at the fish's mouth and hem it (see page 7). Thread a piece of soft wire through the hem. Shape the wire into a circle and twist the ends together.

Crafty carp

Cut out two fish, exactly the same shape, from white fabric (see page 7). Place one fish on some newspaper and draw on an eye, scales and patterns with fabric pens.

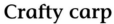

Turn the fish inside out and hang it up with a loop of string in a place where it will catch the wind.

Bright bracelets

Cut five strands of wool,
long enough to tie around your
wrist. Knot the ends together. Pin
one end to an armchair. Hold the
other end taut. Wind a strand of
wool around the bracelet. When it runs
out, wind on another colour, making sure
it overlaps the first one. Wind on more
strands until the bracelet is covered with wool.
Sew on pompoms, beads and felt flowers.

Mum and dad cards

Make a card from coloured card. Cut four or five
flower shapes from felt, tissue or gummed paper.
Stick a pompom or scrunched-up tissue paper in
the centre of each one. Glue on pipe-cleaner stems.

For the vase, cut the top off a small box
and cover it with tissue balls. Glue the
vase on to the bottom of the card and
stick the flowers in place, as shown.

Prayer bundle

Shape self-hardening
clay into two long
pebble shapes. Let them
dry. Paint on faces. Lay lots
of 8 cm lengths of wool side-
by-side. Lie the clay shapes on top of
them and wind some wool around them.
Put four thin sticks as children on top and
wind more wool around them, as shown.

Life and death

People celebrate the birth, marriage and even the death of someone they love. Although death is usually a time of great sadness, many cultures believe that the soul of a dead person will come back to earth in a different body.

Ghanaian Coffin © Jack Picone/Network

It's hard to believe that this big blue fish is really a coffin! The African man who was buried inside was a fisherman. He spent his life catching little fish, called sardines. His coffin is a replica of one of these types of fish.

On Friday and Saturday, the Ga people of Accra hold elaborate burial ceremonies. The relatives of the dead person choose the shape of the coffin. It usually has something to do with that person's life or work.

Every November, on the Day of the Dead, Mexicans remember their dead relatives. They take clay candlesticks in the shape of trees to the cemetery. They are called 'trees of life' and they are decorated with flowers, children, angels and birds.

The candles are lit on the family grave and the spirits of the dead are invited to join the family in a feast. Mexicans believe that this keeps the spirits friendly so that they will help the family to prosper.

On the Day of the Dead, Mexicans also decorate their homes and give religious offerings, food and flowers to the dead. Sugar sculptures, like this skull, are also given as offerings. These are made from almond sugarpaste, egg white and lemon, and then painted with vegetable colours.

In Sumatra, Indonesia, beautiful padded decorations, like these, are hung on the beds of new brides and in the rooms where the wedding is celebrated. These decorations are embroidered with gold thread and covered with sparkling sequins, beads and tiny mirrors.

Ornamental offerings

Design a fantastic coffin in the shape of a fish or one of your favourite animals. Create your own magnificent Tree of Life and a sugar skull, or some decorations to give as a wedding present.

Fantastic lion coffin

To make a lion's body and head, glue a shoebox and a smaller box together. Glue four cardboard roll legs to the bottom of the shoebox. Stick on cork ears. Paint the lion brown and let it dry. Poke a furry pipe cleaner and raffia tail into the box, as shown, and glue in place. Glue on lengths of wool for the mane and paint on two big eyes.

Sugar skull

Press some ready-made icing (which you can buy in supermarkets) around a small ball. Mould eye sockets and a jaw. For the eyes, press foil paper circles into the sockets and poke through paper fasteners to keep them in place. Press all kinds of cake decorations into the skull and leave it to harden.

Tree of Life candlestick

Mould a tree with a sturdy base out of self-hardening clay. Use your finger to make holes in the top of three branches for candles. Make clay birds, flowers and leaves and push each one on to one end of a thin piece of wire. Push the other ends into the tree. Make a person and more flowers and press them on to the trunk and base of the tree. Wet them first to make them stick on well (see page 7). When the clay is dry, paint your Tree of Life bright colours.

Wedding wonders

Cut two pieces of felt exactly the same shape (see page 7). Sew them together, leaving a small gap. Glue sequins and beads on to one side. Stuff the shape with cotton wool.

Cut some lengths of braid and glue a large sequin on to one end of each length. Arrange them along the gap and then carefully sew it up, making sure you secure the ends of the braid at the same time. You can sew ribbon to the top of the shape to hang it up.

Index

Acknowledgements

The author and publishers are grateful to the following institutes and individuals for permission to reproduce the illustrations on the pages mentioned.
The Horniman Museum London: 4; The Royal Collection © Her Majesty the Queen: 12; © Edward Parker: 16; Matthaie Bakery Limited: 17; The Horniman Museum London: 17; © Eye Ubiquitous: 24; Jack Picone/Network: 28.

The publishers would also like to thank Dinah and Jan Wieliczka for their help on szopkas: 20.